For Michael. #score
All illustrations © Armando Heredia. 2022
All rights reserved. https://griefdaily.art.blog

Grief.

"I'll just stay right here
where it's safe."

They tell me I'm going to be ok, eventually,
but right now I'll just stay right here where it's safe.

I'm having a hard time putting this thing down. When I'm staring right at it, I feel "ok", but when I try to look away, to just function "normally", I can't.

I was fortunate to be able to take a few of my brother's shirts before I came home.
I wore one last night, it was too big for my body, but it fit my heart.

somehow convinced myself that there is some emotion I'm "supposed to feel." It hasn't happened yet, so I am constantly trying to feel "it", but I don't know what "it" is.

I thought a change of scenery might help take my mind of off the loss, but it seems like all of the things I like to do are the things we did.

I tend to disassociate, and try distracting myself,
which "works" until it doesn't.

Grief

I am able to find comfort in knowing that this grief is love. It's love trying to continue its work. It hurts, yes, but I'm going to try to let it keep working.

"Are you good now?"
No, but I feel a little better.

I use a lot of energy "being strong". Some days I'm not strong, though, some days I'm just angry and need to vent. so I do. It doesn't change anything, but I feel better.

I find myself connecting with old memories and feelings, it's like my brain detaches itself from the present, and I have to reconnect to the now.

**You ok?
I've got a lot on my mind
Wanna talk about it?
... no, I'm fine.**

I feel a little overwhelmed with all of the thoughts,
memories, should've, would've, and if I'd have knowns.

I have to disconnect from other people's grief. I just don't have the bandwidth to carry them. Turn off the bad news it's too much, and I can't celebrate someone else's good news. Turn off the world, I'll be back.

I remember that time when we...   And then you were like...

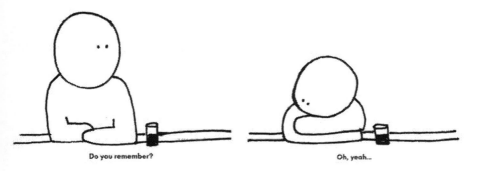

Do you remember?   Oh, yeah...

We had so many stories together, sometimes I
wonder if he'd remember them the same way I do.

I'm afraid my friends and family will get tired of me always talking about how I'm feeling before I'm done feeling it. It's all I talk about, because it's what I am thinking abou

had a dream that I was chasing my brother, Michael through an airport the other day.
When I finally got to the gate, I missed the plane and had to watch it fly away.
It wasn't my flight. Someday, but not yet.

I never noticed how many silver pickup trucks there are on the road, but now I see them all of the time, and they make me think of my brother.

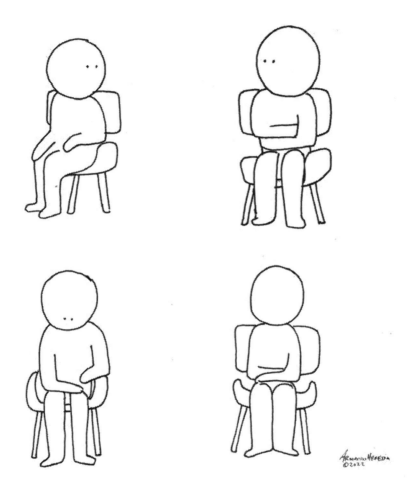

I was with a group of strangers who talked about the ways a person might pass due to the illness to which I lost my brother. It was very difficult, but they were not at fault as they had no idea about my recent experience.

This part scares me. That's the finish line, right there, but not mine.
I know how to walk, even to run, but I don't know how to take the next step.

I'm doing ok, not that good, fine, overwhelmed, drowning and making it, thank you for asking.

Tinakay sent me this beautiful message: "Grief has a way of being a friend sometimes. Hey grief, I know you're here, I feel you and thank you for coming. I need to feel this, and I am going to be ok.

Day 23

I was expecting a more linear and predictable process,
one that followed rules and stages.

I'm fine.

The last few days have been a pull into this ruminating, lost in the past state.
Thinking, processing, and a lot of staring into space.

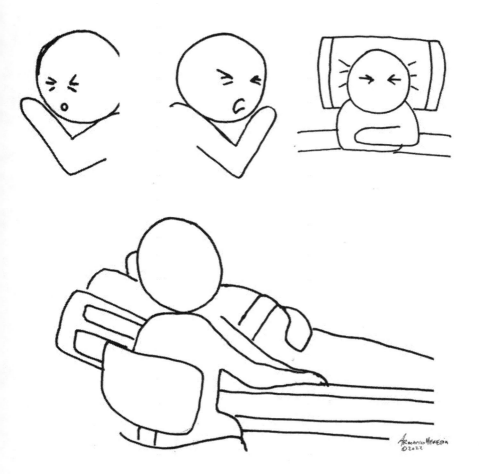

I was sick. This included a minor, but very impacting cough. That cough took me back to my brother's bedside over and over. The emotional impact left me as exhausted as the physical one.

I seem to find myself stuck in a loop on some days.

I feel like I'm running on an emotional deficit. It's like I haven't had the chance to echarge and I'm maxed out all the time. Even the "easy" things are hard.

I'm in the process of moving forward, as soon as I can get up from here.

Tomorrow will be one month.

Grief is hard. This unexpected journey started a month ago,
and I can't see the end, but here we go

I got this... I think.

I'm wondering, did I do this right? Have I felt deeply enough, expressed adequately, is this as far as my emotional capacity can take me? Who'd have thought you could be self conscious about how you lose someone?

Grief is different for all of us. I feel like I'm good, then it sneaks
around the corner, like it's been following me, all day.

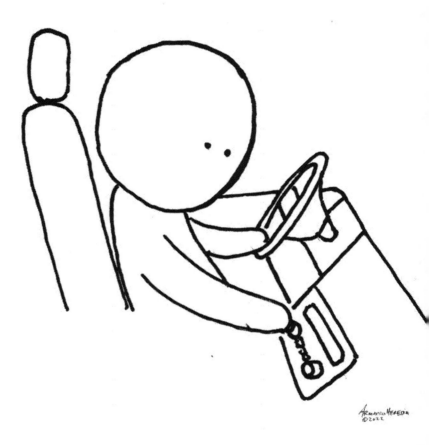

On the radio: "And the load. Doesn't weigh me down at all. He ain't heavy he's my broth
That one hurt, but at the same time, comforted me.
Grief is weird.

en my brother died unexpectedly, I thought, "I'm going to go home and get all of my end
f life stuff together, and taken care of." Apparently grief is not a great motivator for me.

"You know, this reminds me of..." I've said or thought that more
times than I can count. Everything reminds me.

What I wouldn't give for one more Saturday morning of
cold cereal and cartoons with my brother.

I realized that I'm reaching out not with the hope that someone else is grieving, but that I'm not grieving alone.

...e always been a questioner by nature. This grief, this particular one, has brought me to a different place. We're all impacted differently, but I've got questions that make me curl up in a question mark at night.

I'm thankful for memories, and aware of the bittersweet reality that they can never be relived. Here's to you, Howard's in Monahans, Texas. Jack and Diane and burgers, yellow tabletops and pink milkshakes.

When we were kids we ran away to be together, then as young adults, I got too far away, and he drove there and brought me home.
He went too far, too fast, and I can't bring him back.

Grief is big. Some days I feel like I've got a handle on it, and "it" is almost done, then other days I just need a place to sit down and wait.

At four and five years old my brother and I got plastic pedal bikes.
His was the Big Wheel trike and I had my two wheeler.
He was a boss and wore his jacket like a cape.

Your loved ones don't really leave you, Harry.
They're right he-

We all deal with grief differently, Harry, but I just can't.

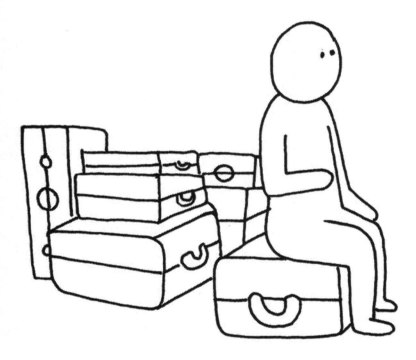

I feel like somewhere in all of this is an answer to help understand what I'm feeling. I just don't know how long it will take to unpack it all, and where to put it.

I reached a miletsone after 43 days of working through my grief and am going to take a couple of text pages to share it.

MILESTONE

I have been spending time daily, grappling with my grief, and not understanding why I feel the way I do. I had a milestone in my understanding, and am amazed at the power of art and the subconscious mind's ability to work out problems and find the answers that are hidden in our own brain.

In my creative time one morning, I was working on an illustration about unpacking my feelings and drew seven pieces of luggage, with no conscious reason, with me sitting on the closest one. I was simply thinking of "baggage" that we all gain through struggling with grief. (Illustration #43)

Later, as I was reflecting on the illustration and my feelings I realized what my brain did subconsciously.

I've done a variation of this illustration before, but in a different time and style, and for a different reason. It was a reflection on when our little family was separated, and my siblings and I were adopted by our aunts and uncles. It was the first time I mourned the loss of my brother.

My brother and I were subsequently separated five more times as kids. So, I've mourned his loss six times before in my lifetime, but always with the hope that we'd be reunited again. This is the seventh mourning.

1. We were split up as kids. It was a bad situation and our loving extended family did the best they could for us.

2. I was told I wouldn't be able to see him or spend time with him because he was a bad influence. This was devastating, because we went from being the closest, to seeing each other at school and randomly on weekends, to the threat of this.

3. We ended up back together, until he left our grandparents to move back with his adoptive family.

4. We reunited briefly until he stayed with our dad, and I left to return to my grandparents.

5. He moved away with our dad to another town that was 30 miles away, no longer a bike ride or walk to visit.

6. He left to the Navy when I was in high school. I was sixteen, and not a child at this time, but I knew that life wouldn't be the same after this, because he was going away again.

I've really been struggling with his passing, but also feeling like something else was happening in my heart and mind. It was this feeling, a familiar sadness, that I've been dealing with all of my life. It feels so heavy because it is the seventh round, and this one is the end.

I know this feels like a downer, but it's been a revelation. Being able to identify this has given me the ability to name it and put it in a place that makes this part manageable.

'm carrying all of my emotions in this cup. Happy, sad, angry, frustrated, scared, all of it goes in,
ut it's already full. So, I'm just going to stand still in the corner and try not to feel anything else.

Some days there's a lot to work with, feelings, thoughts, memories, and then there's today.

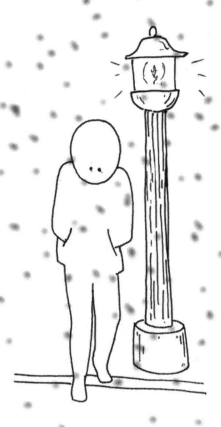

I find that this grief is less defined as it was when it was a dark mass
that demanded my attention. It seems more like a series of
rainy days and sometimes rumbling thunderstorms.

"It's ok to be sad, because it shows that what you lost was valuable." ~Nightbirde

As time goes by, I realize that this grief is as much about learning myself and my feelings as about trying to fill or cover the hole left by my brother's passing.

Made in the USA
Columbia, SC
27 April 2022